My one Book

SQUEAK!

by Jane Belk Moncure
illustrated by Pam Peltier

THE CHILD'S WORLD

MANKATO, MN 56001

Library of Congress Cataloging in Publication Data

Moncure, Jane Belk.
 My one book.

 Summary: Little One introduces the concept
of "one" by interacting with one of a number of things.
 1. One (The number)—Juvenile literature. [1. One
(The number) 2. Number concept. 3. Counting]
I. Peltier, Pam, ill. II. Title. III. Title: My one book.
IV. Series: Moncure, Jane Belk. My number books.
QA141.3.M66 1985   513'.2 [E]   85-5897
ISBN 0-89565-312-5 -1991 Edition

My  Book

This is Little  one .

Little  lives in . . .

the house of one.

The house of one has one room.

It has one

door . . .

and one step.

Little  has one

chair...

and one rug.

He sits at one table. He drinks one glass of milk. He eats one bowl of soup...

one  apple...

and one  cookie.

Each day Little  goes for a walk.

He hops one hop.

Can you?

He jumps one jump.
Can you?

He smells one little flower.
Can you?

One day he finds . . .

one tree

and one acorn.

He sees one squirrel. The squirrel
is sad.

Little

gives the squirrel one acorn.

The squirrel smiles
one big smile . . .

and jumps
one big jump. Can you?

Then Little  finds

one   unicorn.

He claps one clap. Can you?

14

Little  finds one wagon.

"The unicorn can pull my wagon," he says.

Little one finds one . . .

mouse.

"Come, ride in my wagon," he says. The mouse squeaks one squeak. Can you?

Next he finds . . .

one kitten.

The little kitten is sad.
"Come, ride in my wagon," says Little .

17

One mouse jumps out.

How many kittens jump in?

Now Little  finds . . .

one puppy.

The puppy is sad.

"Come, ride in my wagon,"

says Little

How many
kittens jump out?

How many
puppies jump in?

One happy puppy barks one little bark.
Can you?

Then Little sees . . .

one  star in the sky.

"We must go home," he says.

Away they go.

Little  gives the unicorn one pat

on the head

and one bucket of corn.

He gives the puppy
one bone . . .

and
one hug.

He eats one peanut butter and jelly sandwich . . .

and drinks one cup of hot cocoa.

Little  puts on one pair of pajamas and jumps into . . .

one
little
bed . . .

with one big jump. Can you?

He pulls up
one blanket,

winks one wink,

turns off one light,

and says, "Good night," one time.
Can you?
"Good night."

Little  finds one of everything.

one flower

one wagon

one bird

one tree

one mouse

one acorn

one kitten

one squirrel

one puppy

one star

one unicorn

Now you find one thing.

Extra Pages

Let's add with Little  one .

 + [ ] =

| 1 | + | 0 | = | 1 |

Now take away.

 −  = [ ]

| 1 | − | 1 | = | 0 |

"See what I can do," says Little  .
He makes a 1 this way.

Then he makes the number word
like this:

You can make them in the air with
your finger.